Beachcombing

Poems by
Linda Rushby

Damson Tree 2016

ISBN: 978-0-9929048-1-4
Copyright © 2016 Linda Rushby
All poems, notes, illustrations, art work, cover photographs and design elements are the creative products and intellectual property of Linda Rushby and Damson Tree Publishing.
All rights reserved.
Designed, typeset and published by Damson Tree Publishing, Southsea, England.
Typeset in Adobe Garamond Pro
www.damson-tree.co.uk

Contents

Dedication

For my Granddaughter, Felicity, and my Grandson, Stephen, who was born while this book was in preparation.

Foreword

This is my first published collection of poems, although I have been writing poetry (on and off) pretty much since I learned to hold a pen.

Some of the poems here have been shared (in various forms) over the last few years at poetry groups, open mics and on assorted blogs. Until I started reading and posting them, it had honestly never occurred to me that these very personal snapshots of my life and thought swould be of any interest to other people.

I usually introduce my poems by saying that they are mercifully short, and that I don't spend time explaining them because to my mind, if they need explanations they're not doing the job.

Most of my poems don't rhyme, although I love to read rhyming poetry. I have the utmost respect for people who can write in rhyme and do it well, but I'm wary of the contrived 'plunkety plunk' effect. However, every now and again a thought comes to me in the form of a rhyming couplet, and when that happens I do try to continue in the same vein.

I hope you enjoy these poems. If what I have to say is of interest to you, please feel free to follow me on my blog, 'Solent Green', at http://damson-tree.co.uk/blog/

Linda
Southsea, April 2016

I

Life and Other Challenges

Life and Other Challenges

The poems in this first section reflect some of the emotional high and low points of life.

For me, one of the main attractions of writing poetry is that it is the best free therapy I've ever come across. Until the invention of blogging, it seems to me, poetry was the most effective outlet for expressing and exploring the link between the tiny details of life and the most profound emotional themes.

I don't think I've expressed that very well. Maybe one day I'll write a poem about it.

Incidentally, these poems also touch on such insignificant themes as motherhood, friendship, self doubt and self acceptance.

Beachcomber

Come to the land's edge,
where the waves whisper and sigh.
They'll listen to your secrets,
but they'll never judge.

The pebbles roll and rattle
like bones in a witchdoctor's sack.
Oyster shells shimmer
like tears for a lost pearl.

Put down the stick you use
to beat yourself into submission.
'We are all friends here' cry the gulls,
carving up the sky in their joyous ballet.

Don't ask what it is you're looking for,
you'll know it when you find it.
You're home now. Relax.
No need to be anyone any more,
just that woman who walks on the beach.

July 2015

I Have Drifted Here

I have drifted here
like a castaway, to a strange island
and built a life
from the things I found.

This is not the way
I thought it would be.
When I started my voyage
my dreams were of harbours,
flags and bands, crowds and statues.

But I floated here,
to this empty shore
where I made my shelter
like a caddis-fly,
of sticks and stones,
bright shells,
and glittering fragments.

And perhaps, after all,
that is good enough.

June 2007

Love Song for Laura

At dead of night I hear your cry,
plaintive, insistent, cutting through dreams.
I stumble from sleep, half cursing, half groaning,
to comfort your pain and answer your need.

Nestling beside me, you take the nipple,
greedily sucking, hungry for love.
I gaze at your body, your tiny perfection,
your hands grasping tightly, my hands holding safe.

Sated at last, you pull away.
Eyes meet eyes in the purest love.
Your smile shows the cause of your pain and frustration:
a sliver of white in a swollen gum.

In that smile is my own love's reflection.
It leads me on down the years to be,
through days of fairies and hidden silver,
to nights when you'll lie with a child of your own.

The chain stretches on through generations,
spun from gossamer, kisses and smiles,
forged like titanium by our labours,
binding us always in pain and love.

November 1989

Declaration

Don't tell me how to feel.
You may be wise,
and full of good advice,
but you don't know me.

You may be full
of good intentions
in fact, I'm sure you are.
But you don't know me.

Perhaps you know yourself,
I hope you do,
that's so important.
But I don't know you,
And you don't know me.

Please do not think
the things that make you feel
the way you want to feel
will do the same for me
when you don't know me.

It's not that I'm ungrateful
for your good intentions.
It's not that I don't want to feel
the light of joy, contentment, happiness.
But why should your ideas mean the same to me
when you don't know me?

So please, respect our differences
and take me as I am.
I will not be a poor reflection
of who you want me to
but I will do my damnedest
to be the me
that only I can be.

March 2016

A New World (for Stevie)

The world changed today.
A new life appeared,
and cracked open the shell of possibility.

The seeds scatter and fall
to burrow deep
into the rich humus of
fate and circumstance.

Ready to forge a new path
through the forest of life.

The adventure begins.

April 2016

In Dreams

In dreams I fall in love.
Man after man, night after night.
In the mornings, I wake alone,
and watch the strips of sunlight and shadow
move across the bedroom wall.

December 2015

Freudian Slip

I once pared from my life
all the things which
gave me enjoyment.
Because of the expense,
of time, of energy,
of disappointment.

And what was left?
I felt as though
the best I could do with my life
was pretend it was just a joke
all along.

A Freudian slip
I almost made.

August 2006

Hope

'You're such an old romantic' I said, teasing.
'I know' he confirmed
'A hopeless romantic, in both senses.'
I didn't say that,
he'd twisted my words,
but I let it lie.

Myself I have a strange relationship with hope.
I lose it frequently, like so many things:
glasses, keys, phone.
My mind: always.
My temper: rarely.
But hope? On a daily basis.

I try not to let it bother me.
It usually turns up somewhere,
often in the place I thought I'd searched
a thousand times;
sometimes in the last place
that I saw it;
always in the last place that I look.

But would I ever give it up, voluntarily?
Say: 'to hell with it, it's gone for good'?
Never.

At least, I hope not.

July 2015

Two frogs

'Is it just me,
or is it getting
hot in here?'
the frog said to himself,
swimming thorough
a stream of bubbles.

Or maybe not.
As far as I'm aware,
frogs are not much given
to abstract thought.

Suspending disbelief:
'Yes, really, it's
quite balmy,
I must say.
In fact,
a bit too warm,
for my taste,
but mustn't grumble,
I suppose.
Though, really
it is getting
rather hot.'
And on he swam.
Round and round.

Until the moment
someone threw
another frog
into the pot.

'It's boiling!' screamed
the second frog
before he croaked.

'Well, some frogs!'
said the first one,
'Can't even stand
a bit of heat!
Though I must say,
I thought that it
was getting warm.'

And on he swam,
round and round.

November 2008

Failure is my friend

Failure is my friend.
It welcomes me with open arms.
It puts the kettle on and takes my coat,
and seats me in the chair beside its fire.

It asks me how I've been,
and why I've come
to visit it again.
I try to smile, and say 'You know,
that's just the way it goes.'

It takes my hand, and squeezes gently,
sympathetically.
I see its eyes begin to fill with tears,
the tears I won't allow myself to shed.

For we are comfortable here,
familiar,
together in this place again.

I cannot imagine
how it would feel
to have somewhere else to go.

February 2008

Legal Highs (for Hilda)

Pour the laughter,
sweet or dry.
Taste the gossip,
spiced and salty.

Enjoy the bouquet
of friendship, well seasoned,
mature and full-bodied.
The base notes and highlights,
developed down the years.
Savour the kindness
and mutual sharing.

We know each other's minds,
share each other's lives.
Love has many forms.
Take care, my friend.

January 2015

Brief Candle

Life burns slowly, as a candle fills the air.
Lavender, cloves, geranium,
sweet scents that calm and soothe.
Cinnamon, musk and bergamot
spicy notes excite and stimulate.
Frankincense, patchouli,
earth tones speak of ancient mysteries.

Peace and gladness, love and joy,
Breathe them in and feel them all.
Breathe them out and let them go.
Another breath, another life.

Life burns swiftly, like a lightning bolt,
ripping through the night and leaving darkness.
In its shadow they may find you:
anger, sorrow, fear and loss.
Through your tears you feel them burning.

Take a moment, light the candle.
Breathe them in and feel them all.
Breathe them out and let them go.

In the stillness, hope may find you.
A light in the darkness.

September 2015

II
Trees, Birds and Other
Inspirations

Trees, Birds and Other Inspirations

The categories in this book are pretty arbitrary, but one thing that I noticed when trying to sort out the poems for inclusion was that birds featured in quite a few. So I decided to take this as a way of linking to my love of the natural world, and have included poems inspired by trees, the seasons and other natural phenomena.

Some of these poems are purely observational, but in most I have tried to link with other thoughts and ideas: death, ageing, good stuff like that.

Summer Poem

Among the trees,
between the earth and sky
on ropes suspended, swaying gently.
Canvas wraps around my body,
holds me close.

Branches creak and grumble.
Whispering leaves tell stories
to the inattentive bees
humming to drown the tales
of times long gone,
too busy with the business
of today.

The fountain splashes
in amongst the cooing of the doves.
Warm scents of grass and honeysuckle
cannot tempt the bees
from roses, heavy, sensuous.

Through veiled lids
I see the crimson glow of summer.
And do I feel
cool lips upon my skin?
Warm flesh to share my joy?
Here in this summer afternoon, it seems
that anything could happen.

June 2008

How long does it take to grow a tree?

How long does it take to grow a tree?
I stand before the house where first I grew
and stare in wonder at your size, your strength,
your permanence. The wrought iron gate is gone,
the crumbling wall replaced by livid brick.
The house is smaller than it was, and in
my memory I find there is no trace
of your existence, even as a sapling.
Yet now your branches tap
the window where I leant and dreamt of
wider worlds and broader skies.

How could you be here, and I not know?
Maybe you have a longer claim than mine
to this place. Thirty years perhaps,
to twenty that I spent. The Queen of May,
your shining glory will return each year
to light the month that shares your name.
My beauty blossomed once, and faded then.
My branches tend to fruit now, not to flowers,
My seedlings spread their roots in other soils.

How long does it take to grow a woman?
Half a century gone, yet still I strive
to push towards the light. My roots dig deep
and greedily draw the nutrients to my leaves
unfurling in the loving of the sun.
They grow and wither, fade and fall away,
yet new ones come, and still I stretch on up.

Until the lightning strike, or fungus plague,
will topple me, returning to the earth.
And in my inner cortex, sap and wood
I know that I am still the girl who grew
and blossomed in the place where you now stand.

May 2004

November afternoon in Milton Keynes

Winter sunlight
shines on the empty tables
outside the café.
Silver sliding
off glass and aluminium.

Starlings stalking
indifferent to
passing shoppers.
No crumbs today.

Smoke lifting
through the slanting sunlight.
A girl with a cigarette
waits for a friend.

Watch the moment,
from the café window.
Lives passing,
in silver brilliance,
as the year dies slowly.

November 2003

Miko and the Starlings

Through the window she watches.
Whiskers alert, body rigid,
tail gently flicking.
Starlings squabble over breadcrumbs,
unaware.

If the glass could dissolve,
she would be among them.
Yet, well fed, she has no need.
Feathers on a ball would do as well.
No malice in her gaze,
just eagerness and life,
frustrated by the glass between.

So death may be as casual as a cat.
We peck and flutter,
secure in our ignorance.
No thought of danger here.
But who can say the time
when the glass might break?

September 2007

Autumn Morning

Abseiling past the windows
on ropes of twisted silver
the busy weavers
have been hard at work.

Morning mist
catches the night's endeavours
woven through and round the branches,
from tree to house
and back again.

Droplets hang from every leaf
suspended in time and motion.
Waiting for the day to start.

September 2008

Butterflies

Butterflies on their mating flight,
spiralling upwards against a blue sky
until one dives,
suddenly, with strange purpose,
and disappears
beneath the eaves.

June 2014

One For Sorrow

Magpie by the roadside,
screeching like the rusty gates of hell.
Cocks his gleaming head at me
midnight blue shading to obsidian.

Good morning Sir.
I trust you are well?
And your lady too?
Do you hold my destiny
grappled in your claw?
Or is that my responsibility?
Who knows?
But it never hurts
to be polite.

July 2015

III

Love and Consequences

Love and Consequences

What is there to say about love, sex and relationships that hasn't already been said poetically a million times?

I guess everyone's experience is unique, and mine has taught me that romantic love, however blissful it seems in the beginning, comes with a price tag, a sell-by-date and an aftermath. Unrequited love, faithless love and lost love are perennial themes of life.

So, given what I said earlier about therapy, perhaps it's not surprising that the 'L' word holds such enduring fascination for poets.

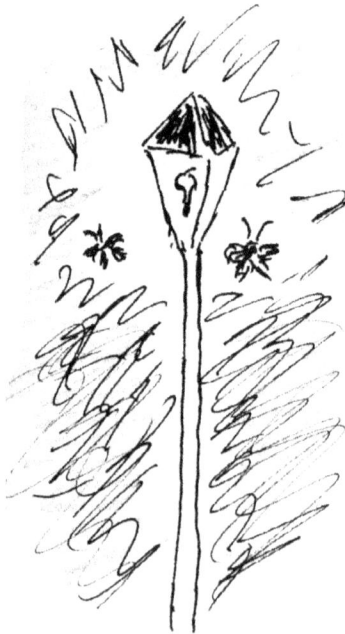

Night Butterflies

A moment, swift as shadowfall:
You and I together in the dark
of empty streets.
My arm around your waist, yours resting
on my shoulders.

No talk of love, just footsteps echoing
among the night sounds of cicadas.
Moth shadows passing through the light
of street lamps' strange attraction.

'Night butterflies' you said
'What are they called?'
Your perfect English let you down for once.
Or did you ask it just to hear my voice,
as I would do with you?

Worlds lie between us now,
and all I have is moments such as this,
briefer than the wing-beat of a moth.
Caught upon the pin of memory
and trapped beneath the glass
of might-have-been.

October 2007

The Words I Thought I Said

Maybe
the words I thought I said
were not the ones you heard,
or needed to hear.
The meaning falls between the cracks of letters,
twisting, turning,
into new and ugly shapes
before it reaches you.

Or is it just
that you don't want to hear at all
the things I want to say?
And though I shout and scream,
still I am mute,
against the curtains of indifference
pulled tight across your mind.

You will not hear.
Your wilful deafness
swallows all my echoes,
and leaves me filled with wondering despair,
my eyes with pointless tears.

April 2008

You Fit Into My Arms

You fit into my arms as you always did,
your face between my breasts, head cradled
by my encircling arm.
Belly to belly, our legs
still tangled in the old familiar knot.
Your breathing deep and slow, content,
within the contours of my body.

Open eyed, I stare beyond
your morning-tousled head,
and watch the curtains, stirring in the draught
from the noisy waking world.
My heart still beats against you,
but my dreams have flown away.

August 2007

Forbidden Fruit

The grapes hang heavy on the vine.
The warm September sun caresses them,
and coaxes perfume from their purple skin.

The vixen pauses in her homeward path
and sniffs the air. The smell,
intoxicating, warms her breath.

She has no need to tear herself away,
no cubs at home who need her now.
So, why not stay awhile, and drink it in?

Above her head, the happy wasps
buzz drunkenly. Their path is clear,
they are not bound to earth.

She reaches one paw, then a second,
resting gently on a lower branch.
And now she stretches up to her full height.

The smell seduces her and leads her on.
Her nostrils open wide to draw it in,
the lovely scent of summer and of life.

Just one more inch, her tongue will reach the fruit.
She yearns, she strives, but still they stay
forever hovering beyond her grasp.

She knows she cannot reach the final inch.
She howls, she cries, and sadly turns
away towards her den.

February 2008

Eyes

Lend me your eyes, so I can see myself,
the way I was that night.
Two strangers, chatting casually over dinner,
until that moment, gesture, word or touch
that told us both the way that it would be.

As dark as my own, in them I saw reflected,
passion, seduction, longing and desire,
the promise of the night that was to come.
From eyes to lips, the contact followed swiftly,
drawing us further in, and further still.

Lend me your eyes, so I can see myself,
I look in the mirror, and try to see them there,
but all I see is pain.

November 2008

Couples

Couples, passing by my window.
Together, enclosed in
their own space.
Where are they going? To the pub, perhaps,
or just for a Sunday country stroll?

Do they speak to one another?
I cannot hear,
behind my glass.
Are there words they need to say?

Do they talk of
inconsequential things,
or tell each other
what is in their hearts?

Or simply walk together,
side by side.
Companionable.

But then,
there are silences.
and silences.

November 2008

For Now

I offer you my body.
Take it now,
for now.

Touch it with tenderness.
Make me believe
that I am desired
for now.

That I am all,
the centre of your world,
for now.

A moment in time,
and I will be
whatever you want,
for now.

If you will take me
and make me forget
this emptiness
for now.

April 2009

Wild Thing

Bind my wounds,
I will rip the bandage.
Roll in the dirt.
Claw at the scabs
to uncover my flesh
gleaming
festering
bleeding.

Full moon casts shadows
through my window.
I am a wild beast.
If you try to help me
you will suffer for kindness.
Feel my claws, teeth, scales,
anger
pain.

Will you leave me
or will you hold me
feel me writhe
in your grasp?

Will you judge me?
I will show you what I am.
Ignore me
I will scream till you hear.
Till I feel your contempt.
Till I see your sneers.

Then I will know.
I will test you
beyond endurance.

Are you brave enough
to hold me still?
Are you strong enough
to love me?

July 2014

This Scent

This scent that lingers
in the air,
in the bed,
although you've gone.
A mingling of us both,
of warmth and joy.
It fills my head
and nestles in my mind.
And if we never meet again,
I'll keep it still,
inhale it sometimes,
and know that you were here.

January 2009

Tangled in the Web

What do you think of me when I'm not there?
To conjure up an image from the air?
The image of a woman in your dreams,
A woman who can be just as she seems.
The one who answers to your wishes, thoughts,
And fantasies. Whose words, forever caught,
Within the hidden circles of your mind,
Will be the one you always hoped to find.

But what about the woman you don't see?
The shadow who is waiting to break free?
The one who lives outside of words we share,
Who wanders through the hours when you're not there?
Who grieves for that which she can never hold,
Whose story is a secret never told.
And do you think of me? Can I believe?
Or is it just myself that I deceive?

March 2008

Cranes

We circle each other
like Japanese cranes,
wondering:
'What would he do if I…?'
'Why doesn't he…?
Each forward step
is tentative, testing
the ground.
Till sudden boldness
provokes a retreat,
regret, self-
recrimination.
Despair.
Determination
to end the game,
to be responsible

But the fantasies return,
and every gesture,
word, look, tone of voice,
is analysed, dissected
trawled for hidden meanings.
Where is the wisdom of age?
Decades drop away,
and all I have learnt
is that nothing which follows
will measure up to this.

June 2007

IV
Stolen Thoughts

Stolen Thoughts

The two poems in this section are both based on ideas shamelessly stolen from 'proper' poets. Fortunately, they are both dead, so presumably won't bother to sue.

Incidentally, Little Gidding is quite a dull place, not all that spiritual, and I only went there because I happened to live nearby for a while and was intrigued to see it on a sign post.

I Took the Road Not Taken

On the road less travelled, it's easy to get lost,
and lose your way, in all the ways that cross.
And every day you ask: 'Why am I here?'
And 'Where to next?' and 'When will it be clear?'
The road not taken is a bumpy road,
and sometimes you may stumble with your load,
and curse the choices that you made that day,
when you turned your back upon the easy way.

But sometimes you may reach an open view,
and from a clifftop, see the world anew.
And there below you see the busy souls,
following the road you knew of old,
with all its street lights, markings, fences, signs,
and lanes that keep them in their happy lines.
Travelling always on the route they know,
never asking where they want to go.

So then you smile and lift your pack again,
following your road until the end.

June 2014

With apologies to Robert Frost

Little Gidding Revisited

So who am I to follow Eliot?
I don't claim one iota of his skill,
but I followed in his footsteps once,
to Little Gidding, under autumn skies.

Past the pig sty, and the old grey church
I gazed across the empty fields, and thought:
If ever I could pray, it would be here.
But what is prayer, if not a thought, a sigh,
a conversation with ourselves alone,
in the absence of a listener?
Just a voice,
that finds a wilderness, a quiet place,
and speaks its truth, and waits for answers there.

So pray for me, in any way you can.
And if you make your way into your heart,
perhaps I'll meet you there again one day.
in the cold light of an autumn afternoon.

October 2004

With apologies to TS Eliot

V
Here and There

Here and There

These poems are loosely linked by their connection to places and travel. They include a trio of poems written about London tourist sites. Given my love of travel I'm quite surprised that I don't have more in this vein.

I particularly like the contrast between the last two poems in this section. Written a year apart, they reflect my gratitude about settling in my present home, Southsea, after several years of upheaval and restlessness.

I want to go to Budapest

I want to go to Budapest.
To ride the tram and walk small cobbled streets.
To stand upon the hill of Buda
to watch the river and old Pest beyond.
To sip hot chocolate at Gerbaud,
eat Esterhazy Torte from a silver fork.

To sail upstream and round the islands,
share cocktails in the languid afternoon.
To lower myself into hot springs
and melt beneath the masseur's hands.
To climb the towers of Esztergom
and watch the ballet of the swallows.

I want to take the train to Prague.
To breathe the scent of pines.
To watch the mountains red with the sun's blood.
To drink Tokay and dance to violins.
To laugh with the hordes as they sweep across the plains.
To lie in the arms of a dark eyed Attila.

I want to go to Budapest again.

November 2009

The Crescent Moon

Oh crescent moon,
that shines outside my window,
I last saw you
reflected in the Seine.

Between the towers of Notre Dame,
you smiled and watched me
walking through
the Latin Quarter.

Behind the girders
of the Eiffel Tower,
you winked at me,
your light as white,
as the dome of Sacre Coeur.

Oh crescent moon,
that shone upon the Seine,
why do you peer
through branches, at my window?
reminding me
that life can never be
the same?

May 2008

Lambeth Bridge to Victoria Embankment Gardens

The tide slides out, and gulls stalk mud below
the green embankment's gothic horror show.
The fat old bell will grumble out the hours
as evening sunlight sparkles yellow flowers.
And springtime blossom perfumes city air
where Calais's Burghers huddle their despair.
A dozen languages excite my ears.
but home is in my words, and greets me here.

Evening in St James's Park

Sunshine on grass
Pigeons, frisbees,
helicopter, fountain.
Tourists feed vermin.
Young girl coaxes a squirrel
to bite her fingers.

Why are you waiting?
It will not come today
maybe never.
You will not lure it
by waiting.
You will not see it
from the corner of your eye,
just the low sunlight
making your eyes water.

April 2014

Green Park

Blackbird calling
early evening,
early spring.
I'm walking.

Sign says:
'Pavement closed.
Pedestrians cross
to other side'
so I cross.

Policeman watches me
holding a gun.
Must be guarding
something important.

I ignore him,
keep on walking
pretending I know
just what I'm doing.
I did the right thing
I crossed the road.

Sign says:
'Private car park'
on the alley
past the policeman.
I follow a couple
down the alley,

still pretending
I know where I'm going.

It leads to a green park:
squirrels chasing
crows cawing
dead leaves rustling.

Early evening
early spring
blackbird calling
I'm still walking.

February 2015

Sangha Retreat, Limousin, France

Bright prayer flags flutter
outside a stone farm house,
while the sun sets
to the screeching of frogs
and a grumbling bumble bee
cruises the rhododendron.

Nothing can express
how miraculous the chance
that has brought me here.

June 2014

The Journey Back

The journey back is never the same.
Even when it's good.
Even when the passing show
is unfamiliar, strange and beautiful.
Thoughts are never on the journey
but ETAs, connections, meetings,
arrangements.

Even when the sun shines on pretty villages,
placid lakes and rolling hills.
it cannot hide the sense of ending
of return, of closing down.

No sense of joy, of opening out
to new beginnings, serendipity,
whatever may come.

Instead, the dread of the familiar,
of giving up on life
returning to the dead hand
of every day.

January 2015

Coming Home

Walking into the wind
that grumbles in my ears and unravels my hair,
tossing it back over my shoulders.
The waves growl and snap at the sea wall,
frustrated by its resistance.

Sun paints a peach-coloured wash
over the low clouds and fading turquoise sky,
as lights come on across the city
and the full moon bides its time
before making an entrance.

And I think:
How lucky I am,
to have come home.

Southsea, January 2016

VI
Short Stuff

Short Stuff

This final batch of poetry features a selection of haiku, and a couple of other poems in similar vein but which don't match the classic syllable count. I know there is some discussion about whether the 5-7-5 syllable count is essential to the spirit of haiku, but I prefer to stay out of that debate.

As there are nine poems altogether, I have divided them into three groups: three haiku which were written close together around the spring equinox; three unrelated haiku written at different times; two short poems which don't correspond to the conventional syllable count and a final paradoxical poem which may be a haiku, or truthful, but not both.

Spring Haiku

Vernal equinox:
a nest on the beech branches,
blossom on the twigs.

In spring rain, thirsty
daffodils lift up their cups
waiting to be filled.

Spring sunshine piercing
through mists of early morning
and bursting branches.

March 2005

In sodium glow,
maple leaves gild the gutter.
Gold on black water.
Cambridge, November 2006

Everything that is:
Me and my cat together,
in the warm darkness.
April 2014

Sunshine on the beach
and the day newly washed in
the dews of morning.
December 2015

Curve of a swallow's wing
cuts through the air,
a perfect parabola.

June 2007

Smoky kisses
tasting of your last cigarette,
linger on my tongue
like black olives.

May 2011

Paradoxical Haiku

I thought that this might
turn out to be a haiku.
Perhaps it will (not).

November 2008

Index of Poems

Index

Title	Page

Index of Poems (continued)

Damson Tree

Damson Tree is an independent company offering editing and design services to authors who wish to self-publish.

www.damson-tree.co.uk